NATURE AND ME

Published in 2021 by The School of Life
First published in the USA in 2022
70 Marchmont Street, London WC1N 1AB

Copyright © The School of Life 2021

Illustrations © Tyla Mason
Designed and typeset by Marcia Mihotich
Printed in Lithuania by Balto Print

A proportion of this book has appeared online at
www.theschooloflife.com/thebookoflife

Every effort has been made to contact the copyright holders of the
material reproduced in this book. If any have been inadvertently
overlooked, the publisher will be pleased to make restitution at the
earliest opportunity.

The School of Life is a resource for helping us understand ourselves,
for improving our relationships, our careers and our social lives –
as well as for helping us find calm and get more out of our leisure
hours. We do this through creating films, workshops, books, apps
and gifts.

www.theschooloflife.com

ISBN 978-1-912891-31-3

10 9 8 7 6 5 4 3 2 1

FSC
www.fsc.org
MIX
Paper from
responsible sources
FSC® C107574

NATURE AND ME

A guide to the joys and
excitements of the outdoors

The School of Life

You're probably used to hearing about how nature is important and how natural things are good for you.

Grown-ups like to point out that an apple is healthier than a bag of crisps, and how orange juice squeezed from actual oranges is better for you than a fizzy drink made with lots of artificial flavours and colouring. Or maybe they keep saying you should go out in the fresh air rather than sit indoors all the time looking at a screen.

The news often tells us that we need to look after nature: people shouldn't cut down so many trees, and we mustn't let all the glaciers melt, and we need to protect blue whales and black rhinos because there aren't many of them left.

That's all true and very sensible. But it is not what this book is about.

This book is about the feelings you can have around different parts of nature.

You know something about this already.

There is the warm feeling you get when a puppy tilts its head, wags its tail and looks at you. You might feel amazed at the sight of a huge tree or be fascinated by a tiny ant trying to carry a crumb of bread. Or you might like the feeling of the sand between your toes as you run down the beach to jump in the waves.

In this book we're going to talk about lots of other nice and interesting feelings you can get from nature. And we're going to be doing something special and unusual. We're going to think about why these feelings are important and how they can help you in your life.

Nature can help you feel good in your mind. It can help you feel less worried or less bothered when you feel annoyed. It can cheer you up when you're feeling sad. It can help you feel more confident when you're feeling a bit shy. And it helps with lots of other good things too. As you grow up, nature can help you become the best person you can be.

Let's find out how!

Aldebaran

Aldebaran
is the fourteenth brightest
star in the sky. It's huge: about 61 million kilometres
across. You could fit 85,000 suns like ours into it. If you flew round Aldebaran in a plane, the flight time would be twenty-one years, six months and a few days (hopefully they'd have really good inflight entertainment). It is 65 light years away. If your grandpa looked up at it one night, the light he saw would have started its journey when he was probably still at school.

It can make you feel very small to think about how big and how far away Aldebaran is. But it's an interesting feeling. Normally you're the little one. When you're growing up, it can feel as if you're surrounded by big people. They are important and they are in charge. You're always supposed to listen to them and do what they tell you. And we're always worrying about who is bigger – who has more money, who is more famous or who is the boss.

But when you think about giant, distant Aldebaran, you realise that everyone is small. Your teacher is small, your parents are small, the richest person in the world is small and so are all the famous people. If Aldebaran could see us, it wouldn't think any of us were at all important: we're all just like tiny ants scurrying around on the surface of an insignificant planet. It is nice to keep this in mind when you feel you are not important enough – a feeling all of us have a lot of the time.

Sometimes
it's nice to feel
small

The Leopard Shark

Leopard sharks look really scary. They have lots of very sharp teeth and powerful jaws. They have spots on their skin that make them look a bit like ferocious underwater leopards – that's where they get their name from! They grow to about 5 feet long and they like swimming in warm, shallow water (which is probably where you'd like to swim too). If you saw the triangle-shaped fin on the top of its back cutting through the water, you would probably be terrified.

It's not surprising that you'd be afraid, because some sharks can be extremely dangerous. But not this kind. It certainly looks frightening, but it's not actually going to harm you. No one has ever been bitten by a leopard shark. They only want to eat much smaller things like crabs and little fish. In fact, leopard sharks can be quite friendly. If you were in the water, one might come up and gently rub its nose against the back of your hand. It just wants to say hello.

Understanding what's scary

When you feel this way, the leopard shark has something interesting and important to say: 'If you get to know me, and get to know about me, you will realise I'm not going to bite you. Actually, I'd like to be your friend.'

Something that feels scary might not really be as dangerous as you think. The people in the new school or the children of your parents' friends might actually be rather nice.

You might be frightened about all kinds of things – like starting at a new school or meeting the children of your parents' friends. When we get frightened, we panic, we stop thinking and we want to run away and hide.

The Giant Redwood Tree

This giant redwood tree is in California. It really is giant. It's 269 feet tall. But the even more amazing thing is how old it is. It's coming up on its 1000th birthday.

It was a little sapling when knights wore suits of armour and charged at each other on horseback with their lances lowered. It was already enormous when Christopher Columbus was sailing across the Atlantic. And it's still going strong. Maybe one day it will have a 2000th birthday party.

It must be funny being this tree. A year or two would feel like no time at all. It would hardly notice ten years going by. You can imagine the tree feels sorry for us humans because we live such short lives.

The tree is right. Our lives are quite short. It's a weird thought, and it can feel a bit scary. But actually, it's a very important and helpful idea.

But how can it be helpful to think that life is short?

Well, it's because our brains tend to make a big mistake. Day by day, it feels as if we have so much time. It is hard to imagine being twenty or thirty-five – it seems so far away. Time doesn't feel important, so we end up wasting a lot of it.

The tree is saying you should remember that your life is short. Time is precious. Knowing this helps you to realise something wonderful and unexpected. You can't live as long as a tree, but you can do a lot more. Your life can feel bigger if you do bigger and better things with your time.

You can start thinking now about who you want to be when you're older. You can decide what's really important to you and what's not so important.

You haven't got forever, but you've got enough time if you use it well.

Don't waste your time

The Scorpion

Grown-ups know lots of things: they know about the ancient Greeks, how to drive a car and what a credit card is. It can be pretty annoying. You're always feeling that you should be asking them to explain things (though sometimes you can't be bothered). They never seem to ask you to explain things they don't know about but that you do.

That is why scorpions can be helpful. Hardly any grown-ups know much about scorpions.

They don't know that:

The smallest kind is about the length of your thumbnail. The biggest ones are about as long as your foot.

Scorpions are nocturnal – they sleep during the day and get up at night.

They can have up to twelve eyes.

There are no scorpions in New Zealand.

Scorpions glow in the dark under ultraviolet light.

A scorpion's lungs are located below its stomach (with us, it's the other way around).

You are the expert!

Outside, at night, scorpions get their sense of direction by looking at the stars.

A baby scorpion gets carried around on its mother's back.

They evolved 430 million years ago.

Scorpions have eight legs and two claws at the front.

Scorpion-related words to make grown-ups fall out of their chair with surprise if you drop them casually into a conversation:

Arachnid: It takes a bit of practice to say: *uh-rak-nid.* Scorpions are arachnids – that means they're related to spiders, which also have eight legs.

'Dad, there's an arachnid in the kitchen.'

Exoskeleton: *Ek-soh-skel-i-tn.* This means that the hard parts of a scorpion's body are on the outside. That's the opposite of us. Our bones are on the inside and we're squishy on the surface. Scorpions are squishy on the inside but tough on the outside – it's as if they're wearing a suit of armour.

'Mum, I fell off my bike and cut my knee. I wish I had an exoskeleton.'

They don't know ...

 ✳ how to make sure everyone gets a good education
 ✳ how to make beautiful cities
 ✳ how to solve arguments without getting upset

But this isn't just about scorpions. Actually, there are lots of things grown-ups don't know much about.

It would be great if we could have experts on these things. Maybe that could be you one day!

Be a Hedgehog!

You're not really a hedgehog, of course. But one of the very clever things your brain can do is think about what it would be like to be a hedgehog.

You would sleep for most of the day and only wake up when it started to get dark – so no school for you! You'd only be about 20 centimetres long. If you came across an old football boot, it might look like a strange cousin.

You get excited by the smell of a rotting leaf – maybe underneath there's a delicious caterpillar or a lovely beetle you can have for breakfast. You don't walk very fast – it might take you a few minutes just to go along a short garden path (you really like human gardens).

You've never watched television. You don't know what a holiday is. You can't think in words, but you have lots of feelings.

When you meet another hedgehog, you're both quite chatty. You grunt and snuffle and make little squeals to show you're happy to meet each other.

But it's very scary if you catch sight of a badger or hear an owl hooting. You quickly roll yourself up into a little ball, with all your sharp, spiky hairs sticking out to keep you safe.

Soon it will be morning and you'll head home to the cosy little burrow you dug in some soft earth, hidden away behind some bushes.

The hedgehog is teaching you about imagination. You could also imagine what it's like to be someone else: a grown-up, maybe, or someone living in another country. If you were them, what would you be feeling? What would excite you? What would frighten you? Your imagination helps you to understand other people much better.

You can use your brain to travel into the minds and lives of other people and animals. It's one of the most interesting and helpful journeys you can ever make.

Imagining is fun

The Flatfish

It's called a flatfish because of its flat shape – obviously! It likes to live in shallow water not far from the coast, where it snuggles down into the mud or sand of the seabed. It never gets very big – an adult flatfish would probably be about the size of both your hands stretched out together.

You're a bit like a flatfish. You'll change a huge amount as you grow too. You started out tiny; you could only waggle your hands and gurgle. Then you learned to crawl and walk and jump. You learned to speak. You got bigger; your face changed. You started going to school. And changes will keep on happening.

You'll become an adult, you'll learn to drive a car, you'll have a job. Who knows, one day you might become a parent and you'll see your own children grow and change.

For us it all happens so slowly that we don't see the changes day to day. When you think about the flatfish, you can see its whole life cycle. It makes it feel less frightening. 'Don't worry,' says the flatfish. 'Of course you're going to keep on changing a lot – just like me!'

Then it grows a tail.

The weird thing is that a flatfish doesn't start out flat at all. When it's born, it's just a tiny round egg that bobs about in the water.

Life is full of exciting changes!

Later it looks like an ordinary little fish – a bit like a goldfish, maybe; it swims about upright.

Then something really strange happens: it starts getting thinner and flatter.

It swims about on its side and one of its eyes actually moves so that both of its eyes end up on the same side.

And it changes colour too: the upper side goes a dark grey while the underside stays a whitish colour. It's great that it changes: at last it can live happily on the sandy seabed.

A Cow

A cow living in a field doesn't have a very exciting life. Year after year, it's just munching grass and going indoors twice a day to get milked. It spends a lot of time standing still and staring into the distance. The highlight of a day might be spotting a particularly juicy tuft of grass or having to use its tail to swat away some annoying flies. But cows don't seem to get bored. You don't see them fretting or getting frustrated. They're not drumming their hooves impatiently on the ground or trying to dig tunnels under the fence so they can escape and finally go somewhere interesting.

No. A cow seems really at peace. It's patient. It accepts that most of the time nothing much is happening.

Be happy

We spend a lot of our time making ourselves upset. We long for things we know we will probably never get, so we go around feeling disappointed – even though we might have quite a nice life already. We look at other people and think: 'Why have they got things I haven't? It's so unfair!'

It makes us upset to think about it. But it doesn't change anything. Cows don't do that sort of thing. They don't spend their lives wishing they could go on holiday somewhere hot or feeling that it's unfair that humans get to wear clothes and they're never allowed even to put on a jumper.

A cow with plenty of good grass to eat in summer and a warm barn and nice feed in winter is happy because it has what it really needs. It doesn't ask for more. In a funny way, we get unhappy when we forget to be like cows. Maybe we already have the main things we need.

The View from a Plane

You're lucky:
you've got a window seat and
it's not cloudy. You're coming in to land
and the plane isn't that high up. You can see what
look like toy cars and houses; the roads look as if
someone drew them with a thick pencil. If you had super
extendable arms, you could reach down and move things
about. You might decide an office tower was in the wrong place
or that it would be nice to take some trees from the forest and
plonk them down in someone's garden. You can easily see right
over a hill to the farms and villages far in the distance. Maybe
towards the horizon there's the sea and a microscopic
container ship that might have come from Singapore or be on its
way to Iceland.

Films and the news concentrate on scary, dramatic things. You
can start to imagine that is what the world is like. But from a
plane window it all looks quiet and calm. The traffic is moving
peacefully along the streets. In hundreds of fields, apples
are slowly ripening on the trees and corn is growing in the
sunshine. There are no explosions or invading armies or massive
dinosaurs ripping the roofs off people's houses. You don't see
police cars frantically chasing bank robbers. Instead, there
are neat grey boxes of factories; there are lines of thin
electricity pylons; there are reservoirs and parks. A
motorway curves elegantly around a hill. It's calm
because the world really is much more under
control than you imagine. And when you see
that, it helps you feel calmer too.

Clouds

Mostly
we think of enjoyable
things costing money. You have to
pay to use a swimming pool or get a computer game or go
to an adventure park. (Well, to be honest, usually a grown-up
pays – and sometimes they grumble about it.) When you think
about it, a really amazing thing about nature is that a lot of it
doesn't belong to anyone in particular. No one owns the rain
or the wind or thunder and lightning or a snowstorm. A magical
sunrise or a wonderful sunset – when the whole sky goes purple
and orange and pink and you feel all warm and sweet inside –
doesn't cost anything.

Take
clouds, for instance: it's as if
they are huge islands floating about in a
sea of endless sky. Sometimes a little fluffy portion
detaches itself from its mother cloud and goes off for an
adventure on its own. Or maybe it looks like two clouds are
having a race: one is gradually catching up with another
– or is the front one going to escape? You could
imagine living up there, being the ruler of a
cloud country.

Sometimes magic comes for free

Sometimes
there is a little gap in the
clouds and you can see the straight
lines of sunlight shining through. People used
to imagine they could climb up the sunbeams
and reach the sky. Obviously you can't,
but it's still a lovely idea.

Sunshine

About 150 million kilometres away there's an incredibly big explosion happening. In fact, it's been going on for 4.6 billion years. And that's really lucky. Because it's all happening inside our nearest star, the one we call the Sun. This massive explosion means that a huge amount of light and heat is being created. It doesn't take long for the light to reach us on Earth (about eight minutes) because light is the fastest moving thing in the entire universe.

When it reaches planet Earth, the light hits our atmosphere, turning the sky blue. If it's not cloudy, a lot of light makes its way down to us and we get one of the nicest things: a sunny day. It makes you feel cheerful just stepping outside. You want to smile at people. You want to laugh and run about. When you think about it, it's pretty interesting that sunlight has this effect on us.

When you get grumpy (we all do sometimes) mostly it feels as if it's someone's fault. Mum said that you had watched enough television. Dad said he'd spend some time with you, but he didn't. Your friend was telling a joke to someone else. But often the real reason you're in a bad mood is just that you're missing the sunshine.

Humans originally lived in warm, sunny places. But starting about 10,000 years ago, we got really clever and learned how to live in cold, rainy, cloudy places. It's amazing we can do that – but it's also a problem. We don't get enough sunny days. So maybe we shouldn't get quite so cross with the people we live around – maybe we should just get annoyed with the rain.

Now you know why you feel grumpy

The Alps

Feeling big
on the inside

The
Alps are
the biggest
mountains in Europe.
There are hundreds and
hundreds of different peaks
spread over a huge area. The highest
ones are nearly five kilometres tall. But if
you had been standing there about 30 million
years ago, you wouldn't have seen any mountains
– it was all flat! Since then, the whole of Africa has been
slowly bumping into Europe and gradually pushing vast
quantities of rocks higher and higher up. That's how mountains get
made. (You can get the idea if you try pushing two pillows together.)

It's amazing looking at lots of mountains. There are smaller ones nearby, then
bigger ones in the distance, then even bigger ones beyond that. It would take
weeks to climb across them and it would be incredibly difficult. But when you
look at them, it's as if your eyes are going higher and higher and leaping from
one ridge to the next. In comparison to the mountains, you're tiny (we all are), but
your mind is even bigger.

Normally you're thinking about things that are really close up: what you're doing
today, what's for dinner, a game you want to play or someone at school you're a bit
annoyed with. But with the mountains you can think huge, noble thoughts. You can
imagine hundreds of years rushing past. You feel you want to do good, important things.
Who cares about what someone said in the playground or how you did in the test? You
feel free. It's as if you've become a giant on the inside; you're so big that those things don't
matter. They're too small to bother you. It's really nice to feel this way sometimes!

(Maybe some pieces of music or songs make you feel this way too.)

The Okapi

Here's an okapi. It lives in Africa, near the equator. Some people think it looks pretty odd. Its legs are stripy like a zebra, but it has a face like a giraffe and a rather long neck. It's got a lovely chocolate brown coat – which isn't like a giraffe at all. It doesn't grow particularly tall. An average 10-year-old could look a grown-up okapi in the eye.

Very occasionally, lots of okapis get together in big groups, but most of the time they prefer to wander about on their own at the edge of the forest, quietly munching a few leaves.

You might not always feel very confident – and that is normal. You feel you have to join in with what other people are doing, even if you don't really want to. Or maybe you feel you have to pretend to be interested in things that don't actually excite you because you don't want people to think you're odd.

That's when it can be helpful to think about our friend the okapi. It's not trying to be anything except what it is. It's not trying to be a giraffe or a zebra. It's not too worried about what other people think of it.

The okapi is saying something really important too: 'It's great to like being on your own.' Our society keeps telling us that we should want to spend all our time in groups, but the okapi is wiser. Being able to be happy on your own is one of the best things in the world. You don't have to hang around with whoever just happens to be there. You can wait to make friends with people you really like.

Just be
yourself

The River

It's really interesting to stand on a bridge and watch a big river flow underneath you. The river's always been there (well, probably for thousands of years), but the actual water is always changing.

Think about what might have happened to an individual water droplet that's passing under the bridge right now. Maybe a week ago it was hanging about in a cloud, then it fell as a raindrop (splosh!) into a shallow muddy puddle up in some hills, many, many miles away. Slowly it trickled down the side of the hill. Then it joined a stream and the stream joined other streams, getting bigger all the time. It had to jump down a waterfall, then it dashed past some rocks. The stream turned into a river. Our droplet drifted past fields and houses – it saw cows grazing by the banks and people fishing. Someone was rowing and bashed it with an oar (but water droplets don't mind). Now it's reached your bridge and it will keep going. Maybe tomorrow it will reach the sea. Who knows where the ocean currents will take it after that. What an adventure!

Here's a big, important thought: you are like that water droplet and the river is like your life. This is true for everyone. You see people at different stages. A granny droplet is getting closer to the sea. A baby droplet is still near the start, but eventually it will go all the way along the river. It's hard to believe with people – that all the old people really were little once, and that all the little people will get old one day. But when you stand on the bridge and look at the river you can understand. Everyone's river is different, but we're all going down to the sea.

The
stages
of
life

A Puppy Knows You're Fantastic

A puppy is lovely. It's got such a sweet face. It looks funny and happy. But maybe the sweetest thing about a puppy is how much it likes you!

A few people think they are fantastic all the time (even if they're actually not that great or not very nice to other people). They're really annoying. But lots of us have the opposite problem. You're so aware of what you get wrong and how you sometimes make mistakes that you forget you're pretty special too.

What's great about a puppy is that it reminds you of something important. If you do badly on a school test, or you spill orange juice all over the table, or you haven't tidied your bedroom for ages, or you don't like your hair – the puppy doesn't care. It's impressed by you anyway: you can throw a ball! You can speak human words! You can open a door! It loves you just as you are.

Parents can be great, but they fuss. They want you to put on your coat even if you don't feel cold, or to go to bed even if you don't feel tired; they want to know how you got on at school even if you don't feel like telling them; they make you go to the dentist and they want you to eat broccoli. (You know it's all because they love you, but it is quite irritating.)

But a puppy never fusses. It never asks annoying questions. It's never heard of dentists or school or maths or broccoli and it doesn't really understand what a coat is for. All it wants is easy things: it wants you to scratch the top of its head or give it a crunchy biscuit. You're a hero already!

You are a hero already

A Rabbit Burrow

It looks so cosy in there. It would be lovely to have a little home under the ground. When it got cold you could snuggle down. If there was something frightening outside, you would know you'd be safe. A fox could be lurking about and they couldn't get in. It would be fun poking your nose along the tunnels and saying hello to your rabbit friends in all their different little houses. Mum or Dad rabbit would be there too.

You probably know all sorts of versions of this. You can all be cuddled up together on the sofa, watching a programme about polar bears. You can put on a nice old jumper and your favourite thick socks. You can burrow down in your bed or pull the covers over your chin so just your nose is peeping out. Maybe it would be nice if Mum or Dad sang you a goodnight song.

Some people think that feeling cosy is a bit babyish. They say you should be playing sports or a game on your phone, not thinking about being like a rabbit. But they're not actually right. Being cosy is really important – and grown-ups need to feel cosy too. It's definitely not just for little children.

You can't be strong and independent all the time. It gets too much. You get worn out with trying so hard. You need time when it's okay to be a bit floppy. When you're cosy you feel loved and cared for. You feel safe. The normal difficult and tricky things can't get to you. (Adults need this too, though mostly you don't see it.)

Later, maybe tomorrow, when you're ready, you can go back out and explore more of this complicated but very interesting world.

Feeling cosy

Chimpanzees

Chimpanzees can teach you a lot about yourself. Maybe that sounds silly because you're obviously very different. You have different hands and feet and you're not so hairy. A chimp swings about in trees and picks fleas out of its friend's hair, but you wear shoes and sit in a classroom learning lessons.

Why it's tough being human

But chimps are our closest living relatives in the animal kingdom. Our brains are quite similar in a lot of ways. For example, a chimp's brain gets very excited when it eats something sweet. It wants to eat more and more sweet things. That's great; it's just going to eat a banana, and bananas are really good for chimps (and for us). When we eat something sweet, our brains get excited too and want more and more. But for us, this has become a big problem. Because we don't just have bananas: we have chocolate and ice cream and biscuits and fizzy drinks. Sadly, these aren't very good for us. We want them and usually we can get them quite easily. (A chimp doesn't have any money and can't go to the shops.) So we have the odd problem of having to stop ourselves doing things we like.

It's the same with your phone. Like a chimp, your brain evolved to get really excited by seeing little things moving around. For a chimp, that's great; it just means another juicy flea to eat. For us, it's a real problem because we've invented computer games. They make our brains really excited, but they don't help us do anything useful. And secretly we know they just make us waste a lot of time.

We're much cleverer than chimps. Hopefully soon we'll get even cleverer and work out how to stop ourselves eating too many sweets and spending all our time staring at our phones.

The Arabian Desert

If you just hear about the desert, it might not sound very nice or that interesting. There aren't any elephants or lions, there are no shops and there's nowhere to order a pizza. It's just all sand and no beaches. So it's a bit puzzling – why is looking at a picture of the desert or imagining being there so nice?

The reason is pretty interesting. But to understand it you need to think about something that feels as if it's got nothing to do with deserts at all: a great big cupboard. Imagine it's quite cluttered – there is a lot of useful stuff in there, but it's all jumbled up and it's difficult to find anything you want. That cupboard is probably quite a lot like your mind. We're not being rude – everyone's mind is a bit like that.

Why your brain

is like

a cupboard

You have lots of interesting ideas, memories, thoughts and feelings in your mind-cupboard. But everything is mixed up: a really important idea about what you'd like to do when you grow up or why your teacher is so kind is hidden behind some thoughts about going swimming tomorrow and a cross feeling because your brother said something mean. The important thoughts are in your mind-cupboard, but you can't easily find them. We're always getting distracted and jumping too quickly from one thing to another.

That's why the desert is so nice. There's no clutter. It's still and silent; there are no roads or trees or houses. The sky is bright; the lines of the mountains are sharp and clear. It's just the main, basic things – nothing else.

It's a picture of a less cluttered mind. The kind of mind you might want – and that you can have if you keep asking yourself the big questions: what's really important? What do I really need? What's central and what doesn't matter so much?

The Stone Pine

This tree is growing in a pretty tricky place. The ground is stony and it hardly ever rains; it's sometimes extremely windy and it gets really hot in summer. Let's not pretend – it really isn't a great place for a tree to have to live. But here it is, managing quite well. How does it do it?

Well, it's being resourceful. That's an interesting word – it means finding ways round problems. The tree's roots have spread out widely, far further than its longest branches, and are gradually working their way round or under a rock, tapping into hidden pockets of water. Some of the roots have wrapped themselves round big rocks, so the tree won't blow over even when there's a storm. It has special leaves that are tightly rolled up, and this stops precious moisture from evaporating too quickly.

It's not just the stone pine that has to grow in a difficult place. Sometimes you have to face situations that are difficult too. But, like the tree, you can be resourceful.

Being resourceful

It really would be better if there were more nice people at your school. But you could think about how you could get on well with one person.

It really would be better if your mum or your dad were not so busy. But you can plan what you most want to do with them on the special times when they are free.

It's annoying to be told to stop watching television, but what's the most fascinating drawing you could do?

It's boring at Granny's house, but what's the most interesting question you could ask her? Could she teach you a great card game or show you pictures of what she was like when she was your age?

You don't get to choose where you grow up. But you can be clever and get on okay, like the stone pine.

The Giant Anteater

The giant anteater lives in Central and South America. Its name is pretty logical: it eats thousands of insects every day and it can grow to two metres in length, which is rather big.

What's nice about the anteater is something that sounds strange. Normally you'd think you'd like an animal because it looks happy. But the anteater is sweet because it looks rather miserable and lonely. It walks slowly, as if it's feeling worn out. Its long nose droops down sadly. Its eyes look as if it wants to burst into tears. If it could speak, it would tell you (in a quiet, sorrowful voice) about how everything just keeps going wrong.

It's nice because it looks as if it's being honest.

Of course you sometimes feel sad – we all do. But quite often we don't get understood. Instead we get told to cheer up. We get told everything will be okay. But some things really just are quite sad.

You could be sad because:

* Summer is over.
* A friend has moved away and you won't see them much now.
* One of your grandparents isn't very well.
* You have to go to school, even if you don't like it very much.
* Some people are really nasty to each other.

* You'd like to be friends with someone, but they don't want to be friends with you.
* You're not getting on with Mum or Dad – even though they love you.
* Mum and Dad aren't getting on well, even though you love them both.
* People don't understand you very well, no matter how hard you try to explain yourself.

The anteater looks the way you sometimes feel. It seems to understand. It seems to know your secret troubles. It's as if it's saying: 'It's okay to feel sad. I know how you feel. I feel sad too; we can be sad together.'

It's okay to feel sad

The Swallow

There are lots of ways of being clever

Every year these swallows make a long, complicated trip from the UK to South Africa and back again. They have to fly over mountains, forests and seas. They cross the Sahara Desert. It takes them weeks and weeks. And they don't get lost. They know how to follow landmarks. They might follow a river or even a motorway. At other points they navigate using the stars. That's very clever. We couldn't manage it at all if we had to make the journey ourselves, rather than jumping on a plane.

The swallow is telling us something really interesting about being clever. Imagine if a swallow had to go to your school. It would fail at everything. It can't learn to speak French. It doesn't remember the special names for the parts of a volcano. It doesn't know what a verb or a noun is or how to divide 83 by 15. It is clever – it's just that school only looks at a few special kinds of cleverness. And maybe they aren't really the important ones.

You might be very clever in ways
you can't get marks for at school. You might be clever in the way you're
kind to a friend who is feeling worried. Perhaps you're clever at making people laugh.
You could be clever at noticing what colours look nice together or seeing that the
wheel arch of a car is a really lovely shape. Or you might be clever at wondering
about things that are puzzling (you wonder why adults argue with one another or
why people have to have jobs, or you wonder what dreaming is for). There aren't any
exams for these things, but they're really important kinds of cleverness.
And once you've finished school they'll matter more and more.

The Arabian Dromedary Camel

Realising things won't be perfect

This one-humped dromedary (also known as an Arabian camel) lives on the far-east coast of Africa. It's quite big: if you stood on your toes, you could probably just pat its hump. It's looking forward to going off on a long trek across the desert.

Our friend the dromedary has a very important idea. It thinks that the journey will be fascinating, but it also knows lots of things are pretty likely to go wrong.

It's prepared for the worst. It might find a lovely juicy bush to eat, but probably it won't. So it has evolved a hump to store all the nutrients it needs. The weather might be great, but probably there will be a nasty sandstorm at some point. So it has two pairs of eyelashes – the outer pair is very long and thick – to shield its eyes. And it can close its nostrils to stop sand getting up its nose (which obviously would be horrible).

When things go wrong, our camel friend doesn't panic or get upset or start saying that it is unfair. It just thinks: 'This is pretty much what I expected.' And as it came prepared, it can get on and enjoy all the nice things that are also happening: exploring new sand dunes, going to sleep under the stars, seeing old friends it hasn't seen for ages.

With us humans, it is sadly often the other way around. We get worked up when things aren't quite as nice as we'd hoped. We're going on holiday, but there's a delay at the airport and we feel the whole thing is ruined. We go to the pizza restaurant, but they don't have the exact topping we wanted and we get into a sulk.

Our dromedary wouldn't do that! It would be thinking: 'probably there will be a delay' or 'probably they won't have my favourite topping – but there will be lots of other nice things, so I'll be just fine'.

The Spider's Web

The power of delicacy

A spider's web is really delicate. If you weren't paying attention, you could break it and hardly even notice – a tiny accidental flick would be enough. It trembles in the slightest breeze. Sometimes you would hardly even notice it was there unless you looked carefully. Why is it like that?

It's delicate because it needs to be. To catch a fly, the strands have to be very, very thin. If the web were obvious, flies wouldn't fly into it by mistake – which is what the spider is hoping for.

When you look at the amazing pattern of a spider's web you can see how clever and beautiful and useful delicacy can be.

It's an interesting moment because normally we don't realise how good delicacy is. We forget about it and think that it's always being strong and tough and not caring so much that's important.

There are lots of delicate feelings that you might have.

You might really like the shape of a particular building or notice that a certain footballer plays in an elegant way (it's not just that they're a good player; they move with grace). You could be moved by seeing an older child being very patient with a younger one. Perhaps a song makes you want to cry with a special kind of sad-happiness. You might be curious about why someone is shy. Maybe you get excited when someone explains something very clearly.

These are really important ideas. They're the ideas from which big things develop: beautiful buildings, books, music, kindness and true friendship.

The Ant Colony

It's very nice to watch teams of ants doing things. You might see a long line of them carrying some crumbs down the side of a table leg. Or maybe a group of them are making a bridge between two leaves. It's incredible how they do it. Some ants cling onto each other while the others march over them. Sometimes lots of ants all pull together at the same time to fold a leaf.

They live in huge colonies, which to them must be like cities. There can be millions and millions of them all working together. They do different jobs – some dig new tunnels, some keep the colony clean, others look after the baby ants. There are ants that look for food and others that take care of storing it. There are special ones that act as guards, fighting off other insects. Some are teacher-ants that show the young ones how to do their job.

So here's a big question: why are ants so appealing? Why do we like watching them and finding out about them?

It's good to co-operate

Maybe it's because the ants are all helping each other. They are co-operating.

Ants think that in a great team you need people who are good at very different things. Everyone's job is important. The worker-ants need the guards to protect them in case a beetle comes along, and the guards need the workers to feed them.

But we don't really co-operate enough. We want to do all the exciting things ourselves. We feel we're competing against each other all the time. If we're going to win, someone else has to lose.

Maybe we like ants because they're showing us something that's missing in our own lives. It's a funny thought. Maybe we need to go to ant school and learn to be a little bit more like them.

The Snail

A really good thing you can do, as you grow up, is to try to be more like a snail. It's not that you should cover yourself in slime or start growing a pair of special feelers out of the front of your head!

The really good thing about a snail is the way it carries its house about on its back. When it's tired it doesn't have to go back home; it just curls up inside its shell and it's safe and warm.

You can carry your home around with you too – not on your back, but in a more special way: in your brain.

Maybe there's a worrying thought about growing up that sometimes pops into your mind. When children grow up they stop living with their mum or dad. Often they go away to another city or even another country. Will you have to do this too? It can sound sad and frightening.

But it won't really be, because you'll be like a snail. There is a shell of love that's slowly growing, and you'll be able to carry it with you wherever you go.

You'll be independent, not because you don't care about your mum or dad or because they don't care about you. It's really the opposite. Their love, their kindness and all their care for you will be inside you. That is what makes the shell!

By looking after you they are showing you how to look after yourself. You won't really be leaving because you'll be taking their love with you, no matter how far away you go.

Cherry Blossom

There is a funny and important feeling you sometimes get when you look at something lovely in nature. It's so nice that you feel you might even burst into tears – not because anything bad is happening but for the opposite reason: it's so beautiful.

People don't usually talk a lot about beauty, so it can be hard to understand why beauty feels so important. It's as if beauty is telling you an important message, but you don't quite understand what it's saying.

So let's see if we can work out what the message is and why it's so appealing.

Perhaps one day in spring you see a cherry tree covered in pink blossom. It looks magnificent but also very soft and gentle and welcoming. Normally you might think that something that is very refined and perfect is not going to be kind. But the cherry blossom is perfect and tender. If the cherry tree was a person, it might be a princess who turns out to be very sweet and not at all haughty. She's curtseying to you!

Or maybe you've looked up on a sunny evening and seen a bird soaring and swooping very high up in the sky. The movement is powerful and also gracious and noble. It's as if it wants you to join it up there, high above the Earth, and (in your imagination) you spread your wings and spiral upwards in the soft, bright air. Normally you're thinking about ground things: what's for supper, something new your friend showed you, whether your ears look nice (or not). The bird is taking you above all that.

You see beauty with your eyes, but it's lovely because of how it makes you feel inside. There's a beauty in you that sometimes feels lonely and now it's finding a friend.

Nature

is

beautiful

Bamboo

Bamboo is a kind of massive grass that has turned into wood. It grows amazingly fast – around 1 millimeter every 90 seconds. That doesn't sound much, but if you grew that fast, you would need new trousers every hour. In less than two days you'd be about twice as tall as you are right now.

Bamboo is tough. It's thin and quite bendy – but it's really hard to snap. A lot of bamboo grows in the forests of East Asia, and sometimes it gets very windy there. When there's a big storm, all the bamboo plants get blown over. It looks like it's the end. You'd think they couldn't survive. But a few hours later they are upright again. Bamboo is resilient.

There are lots of things that might make you feel as if a storm had blown you over. Someone is cross with you; you do your homework all wrong; you don't get into the swimming team when you really wanted to. It's all so unfair and annoying. And sometimes you want to go on telling yourself that all the time. You keep on thinking about all the things that upset you – even though it doesn't do any good. It just makes you feel more and more upset. It means you stay blown over.

You can't avoid having problems in life. There are going to be times when people don't treat you very nicely or when something goes wrong and you can't put it right. There are going to be storms. But you can learn a clever idea from bamboo. You can get good at getting upright again. You don't have to stay flattened.

Bend, don't break

The Clump of Grass

One way to stop feeling bored

Grass sounds incredibly boring. You might think it was the most boring thing in the world. But once you look at a clump of grass carefully, you can see that there are a lot of things going on.

There's a caterpillar taking a bite out of a leaf, but it has to be careful – maybe a bird will swoop by and take a bite out of it. Can a caterpillar feel frightened? Can it feel worried?

Some ants are marching along a twig. Where have they come from? Where are they going? They probably think they're in a forest, a jungle or maybe a green city. What do ants think?

You can see some patches of brown earth. If you poked them, they would feel slightly damp and squishy. Maybe there is a worm just under there, and you wonder – what is soil actually made of? It's quite puzzling. It looks as if you could eat it (please don't try – it tastes revolting).

All the grass stalks are slightly different and there are lots of different kinds of weeds. What is a weed? Is it called a weed just because people don't like it?

There are other thinner stalks with tufty bits on top – they're seeds. How does a seed work?

You're looking down on this little world and wondering what it's like to live there. Imagine there was another kind of creature that could look down on you with kindly curiosity and wonder what it was like to be human.

Lots of things sound boring, but they're not really. The problem is we don't know how to look at them carefully and think interesting thoughts. Maybe anything and anyone could be interesting if you did enough looking and wondering. Perhaps feeling bored just means that you're not using your eyes and brain enough!

The Fig

Pay attention to life's small pleasures

No one pretends that figs are the most exciting thing in the world, but they are really quite nice. Usually a fig tree is pretty old – it might be growing up against an old wall in someone's garden. You feel it has seen a lot of summers. It has aged well. The stem has become thick and tough, but the leaves are large and soft. And the green and purple fruit is appealing. It's delicious, especially with a dollop of ice cream.

Figs can't really compete with the excitement of going to watch the Olympics, or taking a ride in a helicopter, or seeing a herd of wildebeest crossing a river on the Serengeti Plain. Of course they can't. But the thing about figs is that they're available. The great pleasures of life are rare and who knows when you'll ever have the chance to enjoy them. But you can get a fig for quite a small amount of money in the supermarket any day of the week.

Okay, for you it might not be the fig – it's not everyone's favourite fruit. But there are bound to be similar things that you rather like, even if you don't find them all that exciting. It could be:

* a crunchy apple
* raindrops racing each other down a window
* scuffling through autumn leaves
* your favourite shoes
* flipping through a book you really liked when you were little and remembering all the pictures
* riding a bike down a hill and feeling the wind rushing past your ears

Little pleasurable things are easy to miss. But they are important. If you focus on the pleasures you can get quite easily, you stop worrying so much about the big pleasures that – sadly but realistically – might just not come your way anytime soon.

The Mother Elephant

It's very sweet to see a mother elephant with her calf, especially when the little one is trotting in between her huge legs, or when she's guiding it with her trunk wrapped halfway round its head.

But imagine what it's like for the young elephant. Its mother never lets it out of her sight. A young elephant might think it would be fun to go off and explore some interesting-looking bushes, but the mother will soon come over and herd it back.

She's always worrying that her child hasn't cleaned its ears properly – elephants rub leaves into their enormous ears to get rid of any tiny insects that might think this would be a good place to live.

She's always swatting away flies and making sure the little one has plenty of mud and dust on its back (which acts as a kind of sunscreen). And in the middle of the day the little elephant has to stay in the shade doing nothing, even though it's boring. When they're on the move the young elephant has to keep hold of its mother's tail – even if it really wants to run about with its friends.

You can understand why. The mother fusses because she has to keep her child safe and healthy. It all makes perfect sense. But it's easy to forget that this is pretty much the same with human parents. Fussing doesn't feel like love. It feels annoying. But actually they fuss because they love.

When the small elephant becomes a parent it will act in the same way with its own child. And although it's hard to imagine, if you become a parent, you'll probably turn out to be a fusspot too!

Why parents fuss

The Window Box

It's quite an interesting idea, even if you never have a window box yourself. It's the idea that you can grow things. You can buy a little packet of seeds; they don't cost much at all. You can make a little hole in some damp earth and pop a seed into it. You won't see anything for a few days, then a tiny green shoot will start to appear. You have to water it – not too much, not too little.

If it's outside, you have to make sure a bird doesn't come along and eat it. Every day it's a tiny bit different. Maybe you're the only one who notices, because you've been looking so carefully. It feels as if it takes ages, but eventually a little bud starts to form, and then – very slowly – a delicate, pretty flower begins to unfold. You feel proud of yourself, for a very good reason. Without you, this flower would not have been able to grow.

This is funny because normally you're the one being looked after. People are making you meals and cleaning your clothes and making sure you're cosy and teaching you lots of things.

It's nice to look after things

With a little plant growing in a window box you're getting a glimpse of how a parent or a teacher might feel. They like helping you; they like seeing you develop. Yes, they're working hard, and they sometimes get impatient. But they're doing it because they care about you – it gives them a lot of satisfaction.

It's not just being cared for that's nice – caring for, and looking after, something or someone is one of life's unexpected and most special pleasures.

Lightning

When there's thunder and lightning it can be a bit scary, but it's also dramatic and magnificent. Suddenly, the dark sky is lit up by a huge white flash that appears for a fraction of a second. Then there's an enormous loud rumble and crash that comes from the clouds. It's so weird. Where does the light come from? Normally clouds are totally silent – why are they being so noisy all of a sudden?

All round the world and all through history people have been amazed by thunder and lightning. They kept asking themselves: why does it happen? What's going on? What does it mean?

The main thing people imagined was that thunder and lightning were caused by a very big and angry person living in the sky. They imagined that this person was angry with them. They thought that they had done something bad, or that it was their fault that this very powerful person was attacking them with bolts of lightning and shouting with their thundery voice.

It's not surprising that people imagined these things. It's genuinely hard to understand what thunder and lightning are. It turns out they are caused by billions of water droplets rubbing against each other in a special way. This creates static electricity, which gets earthed in the nearest high object. The discharge of electricity causes a flash and makes a noise. It turns out there is no angry person at all.

We do this kind of thing a lot. We imagine things are our fault, when there's a totally different explanation. Did Dad shout or did Mum slam the kitchen door because I'm bad?

The real explanation is totally different – there's a problem at work or there was something upsetting on the news. If you can understand things (which isn't always easy), it often turns out there is less to worry about than you imagined.

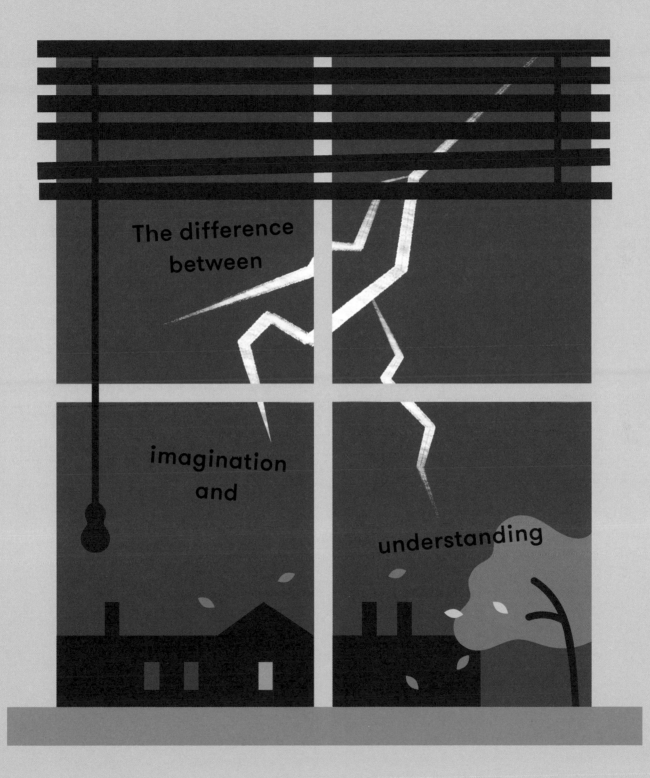

The Femminello Lemon

Imagine
it's winter. The days are grey
and cold. It's raining a lot. It gets dark
early. You have too much work at school.
The football pitch is muddy. You have to put on a
coat and keep your hood up. You can hardly remember
what it was like on that hot day in summer when you had
a picnic in the garden and someone turned the sprinkler on
and you chased each other through the spray and your mum kept
fussing about putting on sunscreen. The holidays feel very far away.
It's not surprising if you feel pretty gloomy. This is when a lemon could
become your friend.

You're in the shop and you see a lemon. It's a Femminello; they're the juiciest.
Before it was in the shop it grew on a hillside on the island of Sicily, pretty
much in the middle of the blue Mediterranean Sea. It lived under the Sun,
week after week, all through the long, hot summer; butterflies flitted by; the
nights were warm and the sky was filled with bright stars. As it grew, the
lemon turned the sunshine and the warmth into a tangy, sharp taste and a
lovely golden-yellow skin.

If you buy the lemon and take it home, you can taste a bit of summer.
It can fill your imagination with the sights and sounds of sunny,
warm days.

That's what hope is. It's the feeling that all the good
things still exist, even if they're not here right now.
They will come back. That's what a lemon
in winter promises you.

There is always hope

The Horizon of the Sea

The horizon of the sea – the line where the water seems to touch the sky – is as far as you can see from the land. You can't see what's beyond it. It could be anything. It could just be more water; it could be an amazing island with new plants and animals; it could be a new country with new people.

For a long, long time, people were frightened of the horizon of the sea. They were worried about going too far away from land. What if they met a monster or fell off the edge of the world? (You know that won't happen, but they weren't sure.)

Then some people became explorers. They were really interested in what they might find if they were brave and sailed off into the unknown parts of the sea.

Exploring means thinking: 'I don't know all the interesting and useful things yet. It could be slightly scary to find out, but it will be worth it.'

Exploring isn't just about the sea. There are lots and lots of times when you can head off and discover things that are out of sight at the moment.

People: We get shy with people we don't know yet. Being more adventurous means thinking: 'I don't know what this person is like, but I could find out. I could ask them a question.'

Ideas: We push ideas and questions away because they sound too big or strange – though they're really very sensible and important. What should schools teach? Maybe they don't teach the right things. Why do people argue so much? Could they learn not to argue?

Yourself: This is the oddest but most interesting kind of exploration. What would you really like to do when you're big – not just a dream, but something that could actually be real? Who would you really like to be friends with? Why them? What would be nice about being friends with them? What would you like to get better at?

Sometimes we get a bit timid and stick too much to what we know already. That's a pity. Because it means we miss out on all the interesting things we don't know yet that might be just over the horizon.

**Being
an explorer**

The School of Life tries to teach you everything you need to have a good life that they forget to teach you at school. We have shops all around the world, we run a YouTube channel and we have written a lot of books specifically for younger people, including books about philosophy, art, architecture, nature and the best way to have a healthy and happy mind.